Children's Music Workshop

C000212135

presents

for Beginning Elementary strings and winds

Bavarian Dance

for Full orchestra

arranged by
Larry E. Newman

CHILDREN'S
MUSIC
WORKSHOP ™

www.musicfunbooks.com
www.childrensmusicworkshop.com

Bavarian Dance

Bavarian Folk Dance
Arrranged by Larry E. Newman

2
Conductor's Score

3

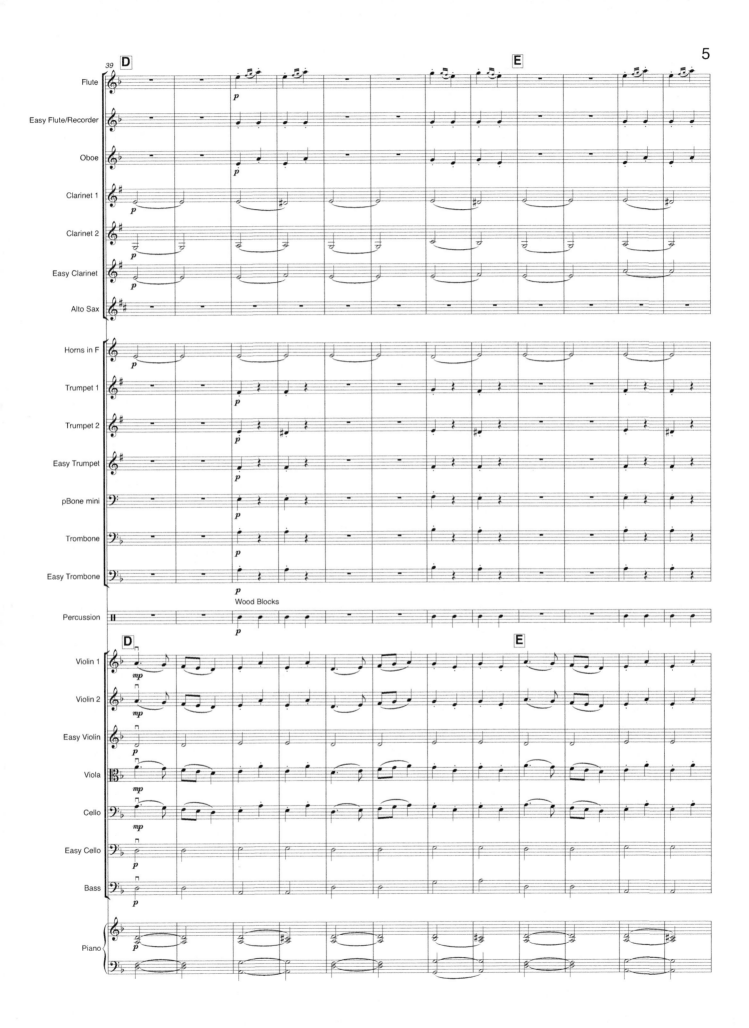

6

Bavarian Dance

Easy Flute/Recorder

Bavarian Folk Dance
Arrranged by Larry E. Newman

Bavarian Dance

Oboe

Bavarian Folk Dance
Arrranged by Larry E. Newman

Clarinet 1

Bavarian Dance

Bavarian Folk Dance
Arrranged by Larry E. Newman

Clarinet 2

Bavarian Dance

Bavarian Folk Dance
Arrranged by Larry E. Newman

Accompaniment track at www.musicfunbooks.com/bavariandance

Bavarian Dance

Easy Clarinet

Bavarian Folk Dance
Arrranged by Larry E. Newman

Alto Sax

Accompaniment track at www.musicfunbooks.com/bavariandance

Bavarian Dance

Bavarian Folk Dance
Arrranged by Larry E. Newman

Bavarian Dance

Horns in F

Bavarian Folk Dance
Arrranged by Larry E. Newman

Bavarian Dance

Trumpet 1

Bavarian Folk Dance
Arrranged by Larry E. Newman

Bavarian Dance

Trumpet 2

Bavarian Folk Dance
Arrranged by Larry E. Newman

Bavarian Dance

Easy Trumpet

Bavarian Folk Dance
Arrranged by Larry E. Newman

Bavarian Dance

pBone mini

Bavarian Folk Dance
Arrranged by Larry E. Newman

Bavarian Dance

Trombone

Bavarian Folk Dance
Arrranged by Larry E. Newman

Bavarian Dance

Easy Trombone

Bavarian Folk Dance
Arrranged by Larry E. Newman

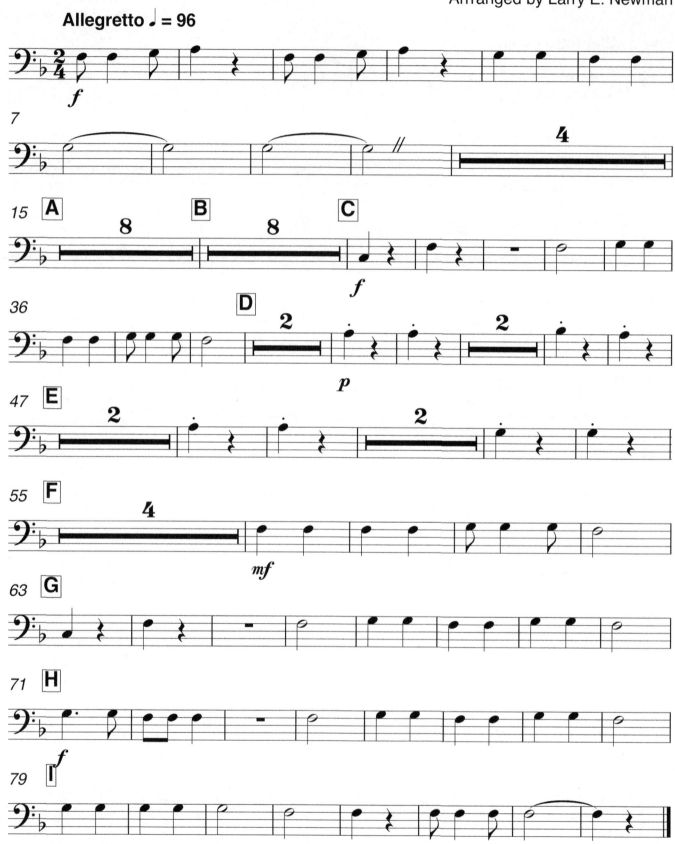

Bavarian Dance

Percussion

Bavarian Folk Dance
Arrranged by Larry E. Newman

Allegretto ♩ = 96

Bavarian Dance

Violin 1

Bavarian Folk Dance
Arrranged by Larry E. Newman

Bavarian Dance

Easy Violin

Bavarian Folk Dance
Arrranged by Larry E. Newman

Allegretto ♩ = 96

Bavarian Dance

Viola

Bavarian Folk Dance
Arrranged by Larry E. Newman

Bavarian Dance

Cello

Bavarian Folk Dance
Arrranged by Larry E. Newman

Bavarian Dance

Easy Cello

Bavarian Folk Dance
Arrranged by Larry E. Newman

Bavarian Dance

Bass

Bavarian Folk Dance
Arrranged by Larry E. Newman

Piano

Accompaniment track at www.musicfunbooks.com/bavariandance

Bavarian Dance

Bavarian Folk Dance
Arrranged by Larry E. Newman

V.S.

Piano

Printed in Great Britain
by Amazon

39689827R00020